WEIRDOS FROM ANOTHER PLANET!

A Calvin and Hobbes Collection by Bill Watterson

Andrews McMeel
PUBLISHING®

Calvin and Hobbes is distributed internationally by Andrews McMeel Syndication.

Andrews McMeel Publishing
a division of Andrews McMeel Universal
1130 Walnut Street, Kansas City, Missouri 64106

www.andrewsmcmeel.com

ISBN: 978-0-8362-1862-6

Library of Congress Control Number: 89-82501

20 21 22 23 24 SDB 50 49 48 47 46

Other Books by Bill Watterson

Calvin and Hobbes
Something Under the Bed Is Drooling
Yukon Ho!
The Revenge of the Baby-Sat
Scientific Progress Goes "Boink"
Attack of the Deranged Mutant Killer Monster Snow Goons
The Days Are Just Packed
Homicidal Psycho Jungle Cat

Treasury Collections

The Essential Calvin and Hobbes
The Calvin and Hobbes Lazy Sunday Book
The Authoritative Calvin and Hobbes
The Indispensable Calvin and Hobbes

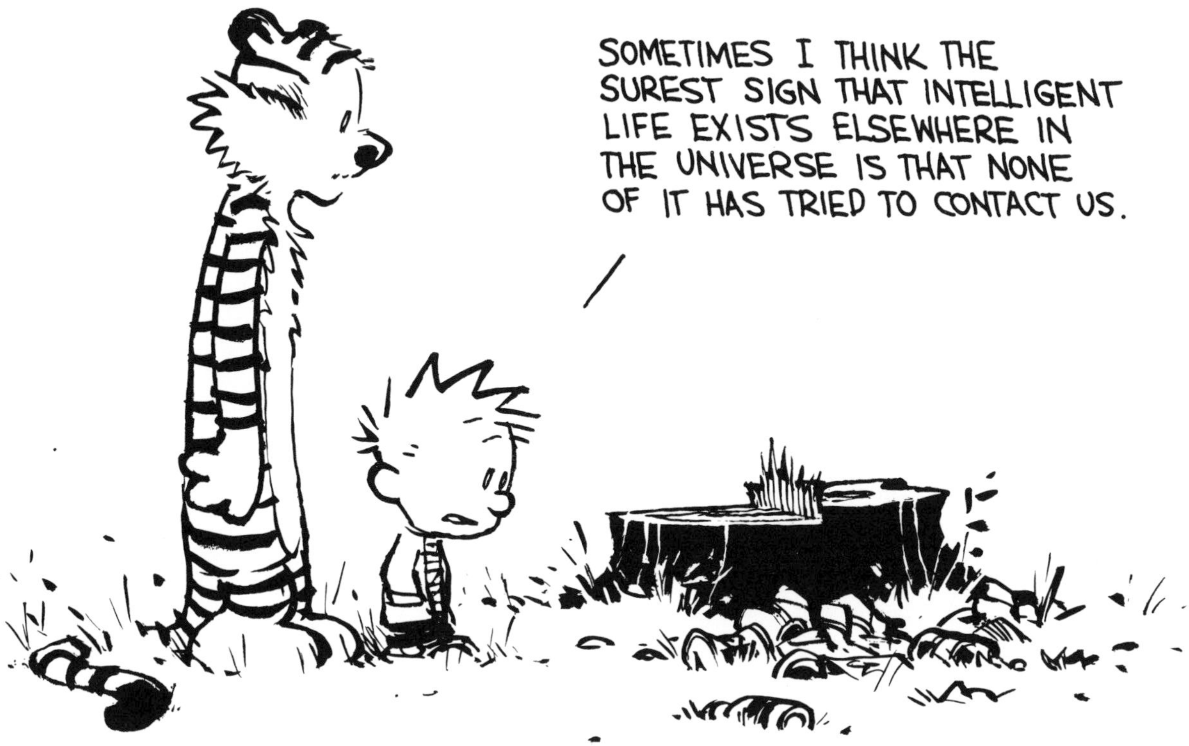
SOMETIMES I THINK THE SUREST SIGN THAT INTELLIGENT LIFE EXISTS ELSEWHERE IN THE UNIVERSE IS THAT NONE OF IT HAS TRIED TO CONTACT US.

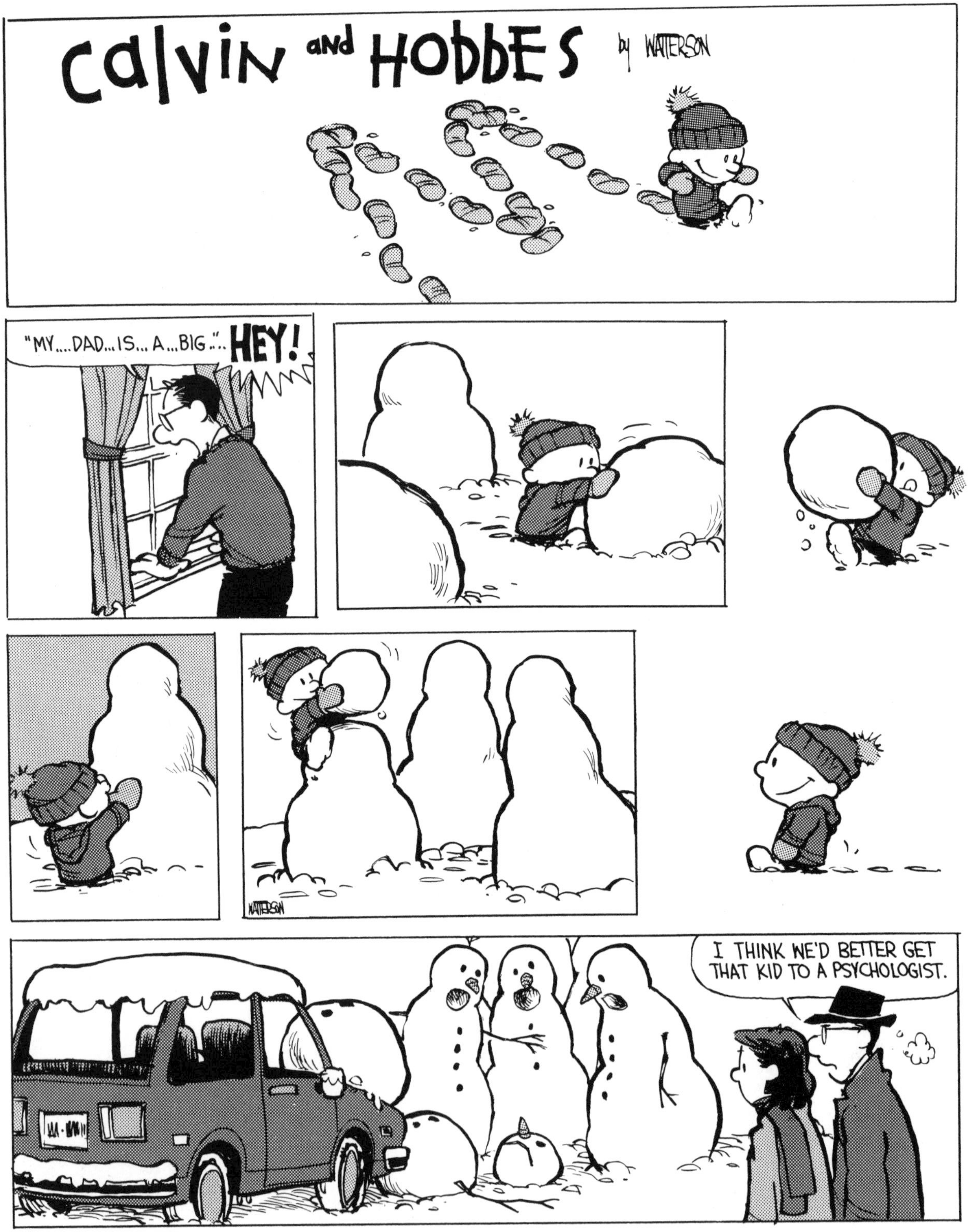
Calvin and HOBBES by WATTERSON
"MY....DAD...IS... A...BIG...". HEY!
WATTERSON
I THINK WE'D BETTER GET THAT KID TO A PSYCHOLOGIST.

13

19

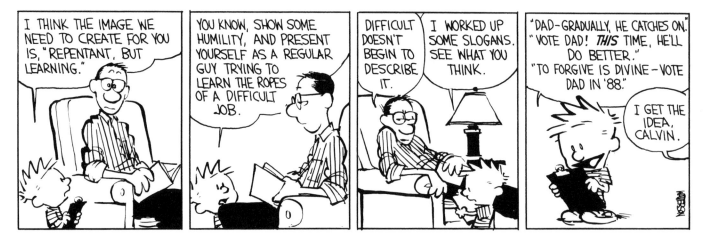

32

33

35

38

44

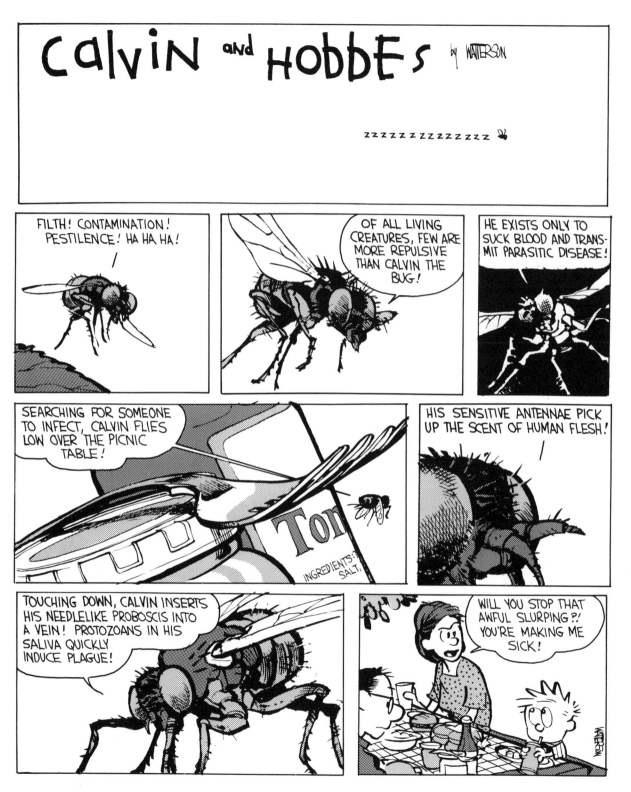

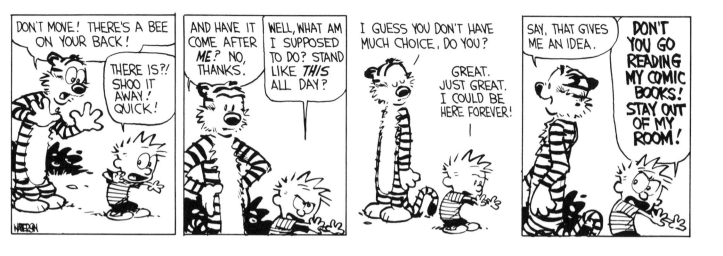

49

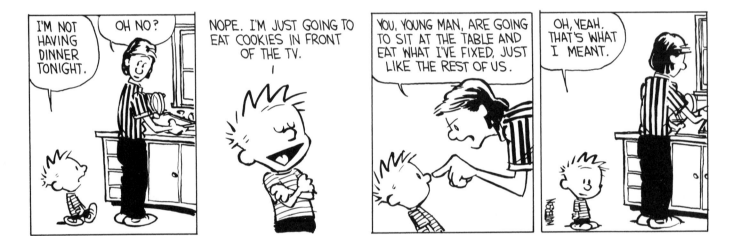

50

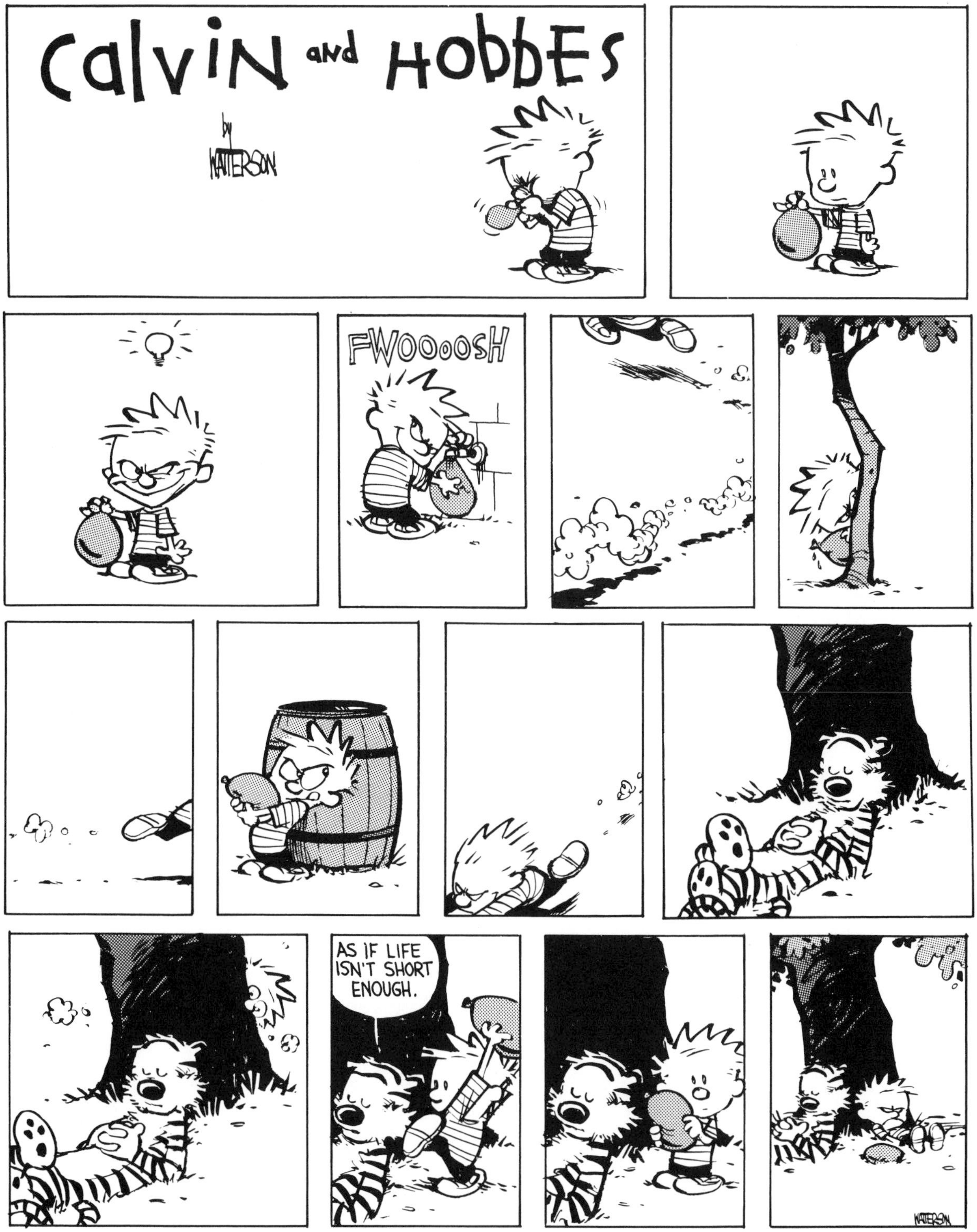
Calvin and HOBBES
by WATTERSON
FWOOOOOSH
AS IF LIFE ISN'T SHORT ENOUGH.
WATTERSON

LOOK, MOM, THE WATER IS UP TO MY KNEES!

SEE? SEE? LOOK, MOM! THE WATER'S UP TO MY KNEES! SEE? LOOK WHERE THE WATER IS!

NOW LOOK! THE WATER IS *HIGHER* THAN MY KNEES! SEE? LOOK, MOM! SEE?

I'M ENTHRALLED, CALVIN.

YOU'RE NOT EVEN *LOOKING!*

WHATCHA DOIN', DAD? PAINTING A PICTURE?

YEP.

WHAT'S THAT THING? A BRONTOSAURUS WITH RABIES?

IT'S THAT ISLAND OVER THERE.

OH.

HOW FAR CAN YOU SEE WITHOUT YOUR GLASSES? CAN YOU SEE *ME?*

WHEN I LOOK UP, I'D BETTER NOT BE ABLE TO.

HI, MOM!

MM.

DAD'S PAINTING A PICTURE, BUT IT'S NOT COMING OUT SO HOT, AND HE'S IN A REALLY STINKY MOOD. IT'S LIKE, I ASKED HIM ONE LITTLE QUESTION AND HE NEARLY BIT MY HEAD OFF! I MEAN, IT'S NOT AS IF *I* RUINED HIS LOUSY PICTURE, RIGHT? WHY SHOULD...

CALVIN, CAN'T YOU SEE I'M TRYING TO READ?

EVER NOTICE HOW TENSE GROWN-UPS GET WHEN THEY'RE RECREATING?

59

63

70

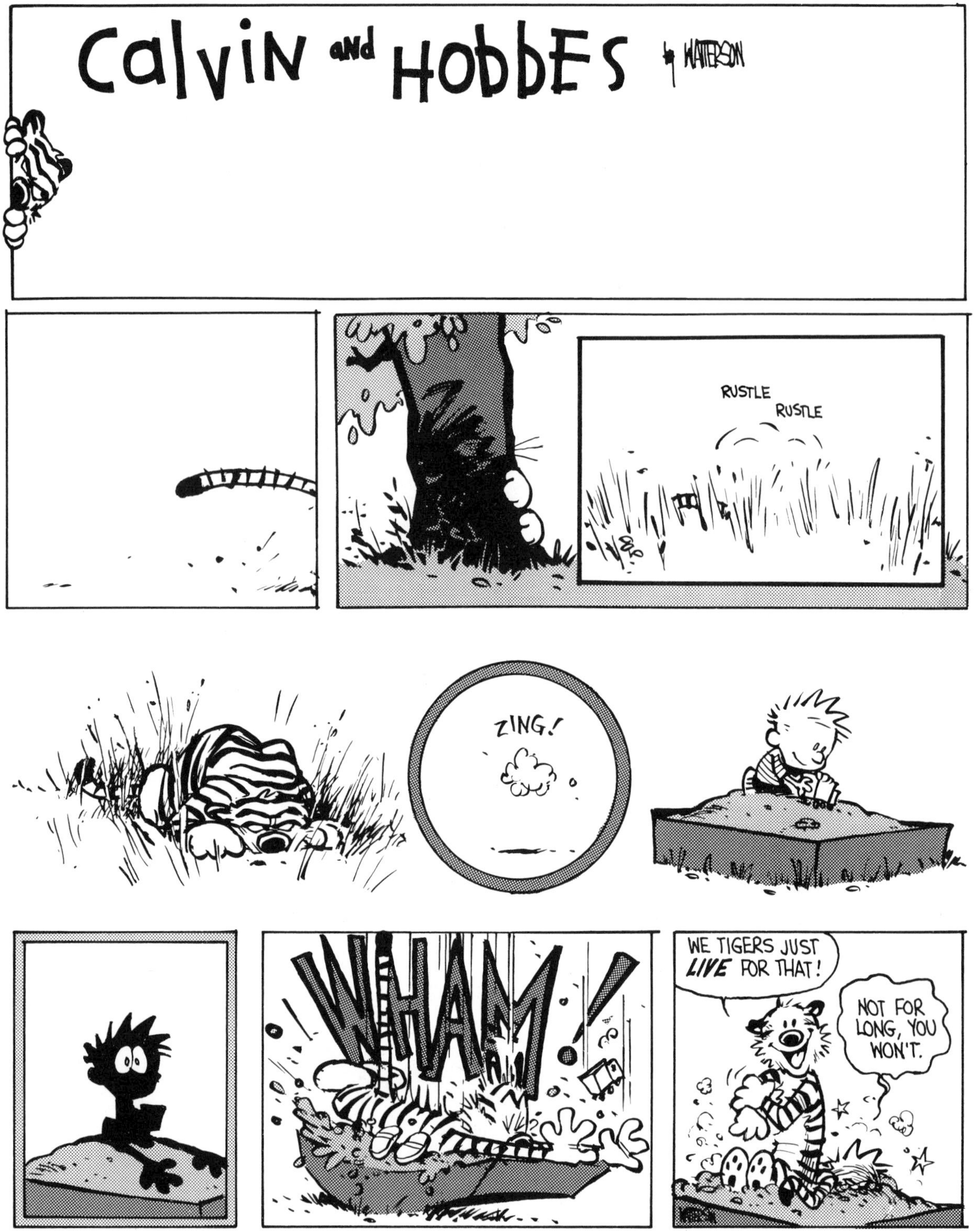
Calvin and HOBBES
by WATTERSON
RUSTLE RUSTLE
ZING!
WHAM!
WE TIGERS JUST LIVE FOR THAT!
NOT FOR LONG, YOU WON'T.

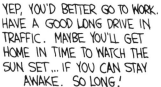

79

83

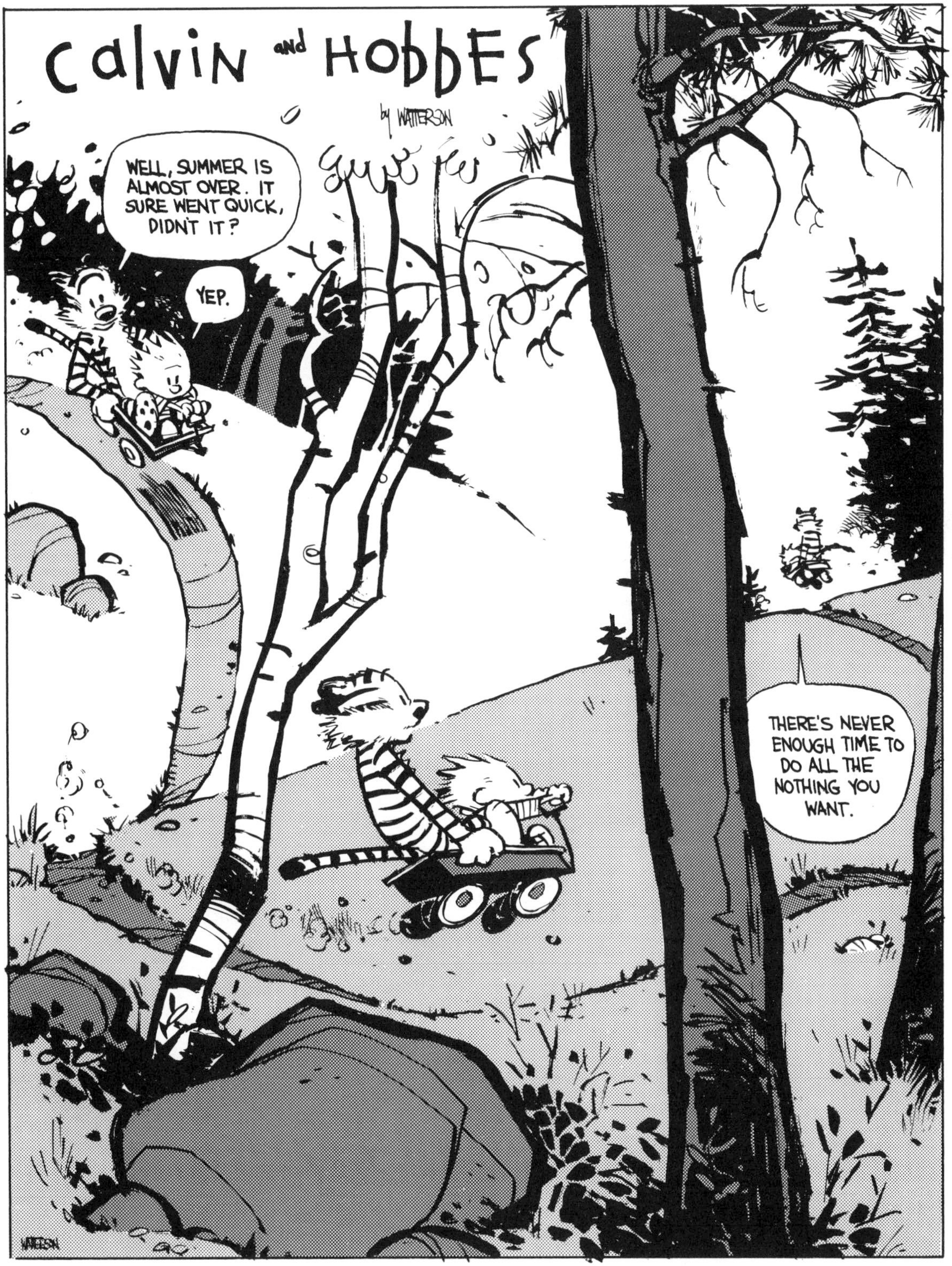
Calvin and HOBBES
by WATTERSON
WELL, SUMMER IS ALMOST OVER. IT SURE WENT QUICK, DIDN'T IT?
YEP.
THERE'S NEVER ENOUGH TIME TO DO ALL THE NOTHING YOU WANT.
WATTERSON

98

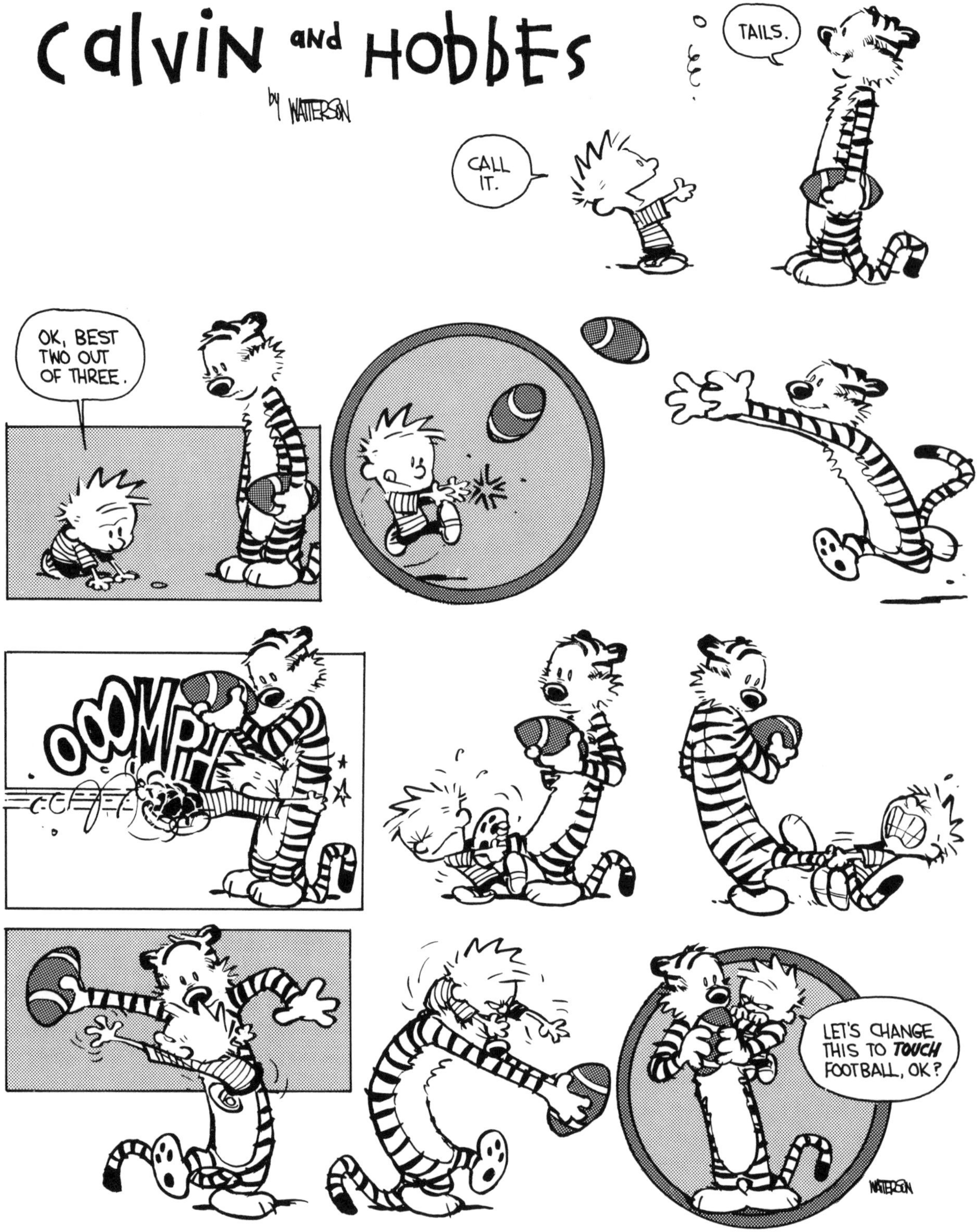
Calvin and HOBBES
by WATTERSON
CALL IT.
TAILS.
OK, BEST TWO OUT OF THREE.
OOOMPH
LET'S CHANGE THIS TO TOUCH FOOTBALL, OK?
WATTERSON

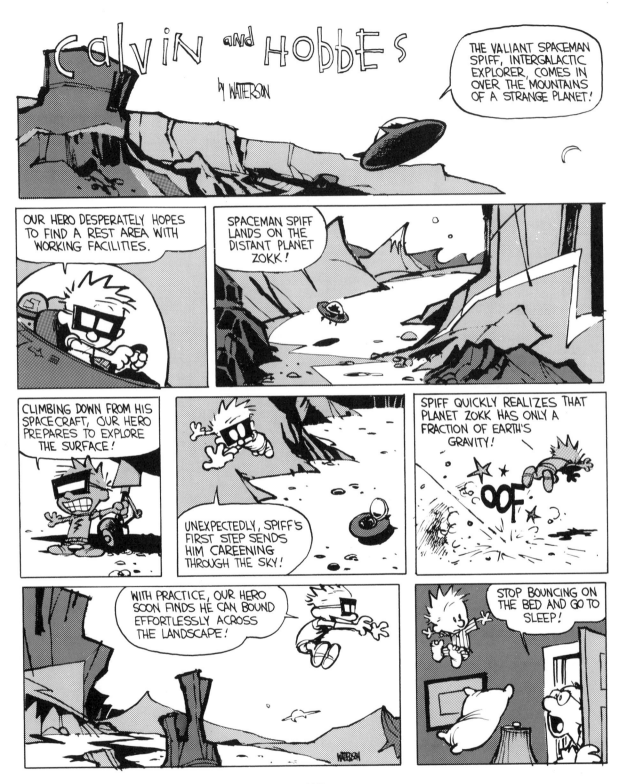

118

119

The End